Towards
Spiritual
Maturity

Towards Spiritual Maturity

William Still

First edition published 1986
by Nicholas Gray Publishing,
26 Bothwell Street,
Glasgow G2 6PA.

ISBN 0 948643 01 3

Cover photo: Dornie, Loch Alsh
Typeset by Dove Typesetting & Printing Co., Ltd., Glasgow
Cover design by Iain Love Graphics, Glasgow
Printed by Bell and Bain, Glasgow

Contents

Introduction to Didasko

One of the constant needs of the Church, and a reiterated appeal from individual Christians today, is for *biblical teaching*. Does the Bible carry a message from God which speaks to us with relevance and power in these closing years of the twentieth century? Does it have something to say which will have practical repercussions in the lives of men and women and young people? If so, our first priority must be to grasp its message.

The aim of the *Didasko* series of books is to meet this need through exposition of the book and fundamental doctrines of the Bible. *Didasko* is the New Testament's word for 'I teach'. We know from the New Testament that the basic element in the early church's teaching was the exposition of the Scriptures in a way that was clear, lively and Christ-centred. Precisely this is the purpose of all the writers who will share in this series of books.

Most, but not all, of the books in the *Didasko* Series are in the form of straightforward biblical exposition. They are not technical commentaries. Rather they explain the meaning of the biblical text and provide application of it to the Christian life. The contributors to this series are mainly men with considerable personal Christian experience and years of pastoral experience working with and helping Christians to understand the gospel more fully and to live in obedience to it.

It is the conviction of the publisher, contributors and the general editor of the *Didasko* series that there is a great need for the kind of literature which this series represents. Their hope is that these books will contribute to meeting that need and will give instruction, challenge and encouragement to Christians throughout the world.

Foreword

In the history of the Church, the length of a book has never been an accurate gauge of its importance or influence. While the Christian centuries have witnessed the appearance of weighty tones of great significance, often shorter books, written simply and directly for the people of God, have had enormous influence. Think of the impact of such 'booklets' as Martin Luther's *Freedom of a Christian Man* which affected the whole of Europe, or the little-known Scot, Henry Scougal's *Life of God in the Soul of Man*, which influenced George Whitefield and through him the entire English-speaking world.

Towards Spiritual Maturity is such a book. It is small in size, but seed-like in nature. From its teaching strong and healthy Christian lives may be developed. First written in 1957 from notes of various convention addresses and frequently published privately since then, it has proved its worth already to the small numbers of several generations of Christians who have read it.

These pages contain the distilled essence of William Still's preaching and pastoral ministry, now extended through four complete decades, as minister of Gilcomston South Church, Aberdeen. The strength of *Towards Spiritual Maturity* is not simply the uniqueness of its author or his style. It lies in his emphasis on the three-fold dimension of the work of Christ. Not only did Christ die to provide forgiveness, but also to bring deliverance from the reign of sin (in Wesley's words, to 'break the power of cancelled sin, and set the prisoner free'). But further, as these pages underline, Christ came to unmask and to paralyse the Evil one, and to set us free from his malignant influence. As the author shows, too often Christians have focussed on one, or at best, two of these dimensions. To that extent the grace and power of Christ have been minimised, and the joy and victory of Christian living has been correspondingly weakened.

Towards Spiritual Maturity seeks to redress this imbalance.

For many readers, *Towards Spiritual Maturity* will serve as a key to open the treasure store of good things. It is a book to be read and re-read, to be pondered frequently, applied constantly, and shared with others.

Sinclair B Ferguson: Series Editor
Westminster Theological Seminary
Philadelphia U.S.A.

1

He is our Peace

The fundamental blessing of salvation is peace. From it flow all God's richer blessings of love, joy and glory. It is not only the foundation stone of the Christian life, 'the peace of God which passes all understanding' (Phil. 4:7), but also the top stone, 'the peace of God which presides in our hearts' (Col. 3:15). But before we consider 'the peace of God' (Phil. 4:7) we must consider the nature of 'the God of peace' (Phil. 4:9) whose work in men's hearts is to make peace — first his person, *then* his work.

God is the God of peace. He is at peace, in, and with himself. A fundamental implication of the Holy Scriptures is that the triune God was, is, and ever shall be in perfect accord with himself, person with person, office with office, and that he is satisfied with himself in the fulness and perfection of his wisdom, love, and power. When infinite intelligence finds infinite perfections in itself, infinite stability and integrity of character are assured. This integrity is simply another name for God's righteousness, or rightness.

The righteous nature and character of God is, by implication, expressed in the demands he makes upon men in the Ten Commandments. The tablets written with the finger of God are the focus of his Shekinah glory which hovered over the Tabernable in the wilderness. The rays of the Lord's glorious light were shining down upon them, pointing to them. Beyond his laws, we see the character of the God who gave them. The laws tell us what God is like. They also imply that since God is like this, holy and righteous, he desires his creatures to be like this also.

We know that God is love. But his character is often expressed in the Scriptures in terms of righteousness (*e.g.* the theme of Romans). This righteousness is no mere rule, or form, but is of the essence of his being. Righteousness with God is not only a rule, but his life and his passion. He is not only righteous himself, but loves righteousness. He rejoices in it so much that he desires righteousness for his creatures, and that, not only for its own sake as a seed, but for its fruit which is peace (Is. 32:17; Heb. 12:11).

But we do not say that God is only righteousness. The Bible does not say that, but assumes that righteousness belongs to the divine heart as well as to the divine mind. Although in Exodus 20 we see the righteousness, holiness, and wrath of God at their sternest (God cannot look upon sin, Hab. 1:13; 'the soul that sinneth, it shall die', Ezek. 18:4), yet, wonder of wonders, embedded in the most alarming chapter of the Old Testament we find mercy and love. What a discovery this is, there! The God who gives the commandments is first of all the Saviour who has delivered his people from bondage (Ex. 20:1-2). The heart of God which burns with righteousness and holiness also burns with love and mercy, grace and forgiveness. He who is righteous, and desires righteousness for his children, makes them righteous by imputation and by impartation through his redeeming love. To our amazement we discover that the rock of his law and truth which is so hard on the surface, is molten underneath with his love.

But, having ventured to consider the 'God of peace' with a view to considering the 'peace of God', we unconsciously slip from the one to the other. This is not surprising, for what God is by the energies of his divine nature, he necessarily desires to impart to his creatures.

It is astonishing that studies of the work of Christ have not yielded clearer and more systematic distinctions between the different dimensions of the work of his death. Evangelical Christianity does distinguish between sins and sin, fruit and root; but the third dimension, the work of Satan, is seldom acknowledged, even where Satan and his work are recognised. Yet for a total unmasking of evil in the human heart the third dimension is necessary, since the person and work of the devil is the greatest hindrance to mature Christianity. Satan loves it so. That is doubtless why it is so, and why so many are suspicious of talk about the devil and demons. Yet it is a strange blindness with which the god of this world has blinded so many professing Christians (2 Cor. 4:4). We propose to challenge it by setting forth in sequence the three dimensions of the work of the death of Christ.

2

The First Dimension of the Cross

The Removal of Sins

We have already said that what God is by the energies of his divine nature, he necessarily desires to impart to his creatures. How does he do so? That is our first theme.

Those who review the history of the doctrine of Christ's atonement generally conclude that no single view covers its whole range. But some views are nearer the heart of the truth than others, in which the greater includes the lesser. For example, it is not wrong to regard the death of Christ as the supreme example of sacrificial love; but his death is more than that. Failure to see this accounts for the spiritual listlessness of many who hold a mere exemplary view as the whole truth. For the death of Christ is no mere display of love in action. It is the putting away of the sins which set up a barrier to the very possibility of love between God and man. It is not only an exhibition, but a removal. Indeed it is more a removal than an exhibition, for it is one thing to show sinners what they ought to do, and quite another to do it for them when they are helpless to do anything for themselves. We need not only pictures, but power; not only diagrams, but dynamic. This we have in the death of Christ, which is nothing if not an actual, factual, objective putting away of our sins.

Let us look at the fact as plainly stated in Scripture. Isaiah 53:6 tells us that whereas, 'all we like sheep have gone astray', 'the Lord has laid on him the iniquity of us all'. Paul corroborates this in Romans 4:7, 8. when he quotes from Psalm 32: 'Blessed are they whose transgressions are forgiven (removed), whose sins are covered; blessed is the man whose sin the Lord will never count against him' and 4:25: '(Jesus our Lord) was delivered over to death for our sins'. Peter says: 'He himself bare our sins in his own body on the tree' (1 Pet. 2:24). There is no evading the plain and repeated words of Scripture: Christ took our sins.

But John 1:29 takes it a step further: the Baptist declares that the Lamb of God, on whom our sins are laid, takes them *away*. Do we question this? Let the Bible answer our questions: 'I have swept away your offences like a cloud, your sins like the morning mist' (Is. 44:22). 'You have put all my sins behind your back' (Is. 38:17) 'You will again have compassion on us; you will tread our sins underfoot; and hurl all our iniquities into the depths of the sea' (Mic. 7:19). 'As far as the east is from the west, so far has he removed our transgressions from us' (Ps. 103:12) 'This is the covenant I will make with them after that time says the Lord. I will put my laws in their hearts, and I will write them on their minds. Their sins and lawless acts I will remember no more (Heb. 10:16, 17; also Jer. 31:33, 34).

Thus Christ takes our place, and bears our sins with their guilt, punishment and shame 'in his own body on the tree', and on the third day rises without them, so that they are gone, for ever. Every sin we have committed, from life's beginning to its end, is *for ever* put away, never to be brought against us again. Christ the sinless One is God's appointed substitute 'Criminal', to take our place. He is God's 'Dustman', carrying away man's filth with his own pure hands. What unutterable love, in action!

Objection may be raised to the assertion that God forgives sins before they are committed. But, it is as simple as this, that no question of penalty and eternal separation from God can be raised in respect of a forgiven sinner in a state of grace.

Two things must be distinguished: God's dealing with sinners, and his dealing with saints. Conversion necessarily involves the once-for-all forgiveness (removal) of sins. But it involves much more. By it the believer is declared to be righteous in Christ, having been brought to new birth. He is not sinless, yet: as John says, the seed of God dwells within him and he cannot sin (1 Jn. 3:9). Because his mind and will are united to Christ his attitude to sin is radically altered. The enmity and rebellion against God are slain, and sin is no longer a cause of wilful pride and perverse pleasure, but a cause of sorrow, shame and self-loathing.

Thus, God's attitude towards saints in their sins is different from his attitude towards sinners in their sins (although he hates sin equally in both — more in saints!). But further, the saints' own attitude to their sins is different from sinners' attitude to their sins. There are no penal consequences of sin after conversion, for the child of God is in a state of grace, and although chastisement may be severe, he knows he is free from final condemnation (Rom. 8:1). If we cannot lay this great stone of eternal peace at the foundation of our Christian life, what assurance have we that anything we may build upon it will stand?

But, are not the sins of the saints serious? Yes, indeed! They cause estrangement between the Father and his children. And while God will not disown them, however provocative they may be (the history of Israel proves this

— see Hosea 11), he withdraws from them — even while he stands firm on the verities of forgiveness, justification and sanctification — and refuses to have active fellowship with them. The Father remains their Father and the children remain his children, but there is no communication until sin is confessed and repented of, and cleansing and fellowship sought. This is set forth clearly and fully in 1 John 1:6 — 2:2, and careful study of the passage should end all confusion as to the two forgivenesses, once-for-all for sinners concerning penalty, and daily for saints to preserve fellowship. Both forgivenesses are provided for in the death of Christ, who is the Mediator and Saviour of the sinner, and the Advocate of the saint.

Roman Catholics distinguish between mortal and venial sins, and we may recognise this distinction if we know what it means, for the true child of God cannot sin a mortal sin, since all his penalty is paid by Christ. Yet child of God though he be, he cannot have blessed communion with the Father while he remains in a state of disobedience and unrepentance. But we have continual access to the Father through the advocacy of Christ our great High Priest, who 'always lives to intercede' for us, and we ought thereby to learn to keep 'short accounts with God'. This is what John calls 'walking in the light' (1 Jn. 1:7). It is, of course, assumed that the saint knows himself to be a saint, although prone to fall. Yet the claim to be a child of God goes ill with a lack of Christ-likeness. It is by our fruits, not our roots which are not commonly open to sight, that we are seen to be the children of God.

3

The Second Dimension of the Cross

Sin's Reign Overthrown

The second dimension of Christ's redeeming work is his death *to* sin. He not only died *for* our sins to take them away, but died to sin's dominion, to defeat it for us in order that the root as well as the fruit of sin might be destroyed. Paul says to the Corinthians that 'God made Christ who had no sin to be sin for us; so that in him we might become the righteousness of God (2 Cor. 5:21). Some scholars discredit this verse as revolting and unthinkable; but it does not stand by itself. Paul says to the Romans, God sending 'his own Son in the likeness of the flesh of sin, and for sin, condemned sin in the flesh' (Rom. 8:3 R.S.V.).

This second dimension of the work of Christ is far from easy to understand, and determined efforts are necessary to think through the paradoxes involved. To help us we can employ the old distinctions of fact, faith, and feeling. If we do not build our Christian doctrine upon the *facts*, and rest our *faith* in them, our wayward *feelings* will never be brought into captivity to Christ. It is one thing to know that Christ has dealt with our sins (the things we have done wrong in thought, word and deed), but quite another to believe that Christ on the Cross dealt with the dominion, or reign of sin, and that finally.

We start from the facts. There are but two orders of mankind, Adam and Christ (Rom. 5:12-21). Adam fell away to God's enemy and was lost. Jesus the second (or last) Adam (1 Cor. 15:22, 45), who came to overthrow the reign of sin inaugurated by the First Adam that he might in exchange give his own holy nature, the new and true humanity. We must not think of our salvation as less than a complete exchange, for there is nothing good in fallen Adam, he is totally and incurably corrupt in all his parts and passions. There is therefore no hope for him; death is the only 'cure', for it is by death only that Adam can be saved from his fallen self and become a new creation. This is what Christ has done for Adam. He took his place, not only as his Substitute to take away his sins, but as his Representative to crucify his fallen nature, that in his sinless body he might slay and remove the old, and by his resurrection replace it with the new.

The ground of this truth is in Romans 6:3-8. There, Paul repeats the truth verse after verse in varying forms of words: we are 'baptised into his death'; we are 'buried with him by baptism into death'; we are 'planted together in the likeness of his death'; 'our old man was crucified with him'; 'he that is dead has been justified from sin'; we are 'dead with Christ'. Could anything be more plain? Paul says that when Jesus died, we died with him. The negro spiritual is not wrong when it asks, 'Were you there when they crucified my Lord?' We were all there.

But we must take time to ponder it. Does it mean that when Jesus died on the Cross we all died to sin with him, before we were born? The answer can only be, 'Yes', although the actualising of the fact awaits our birth and our conversion. The only way to grapple with the fact is to let its incredible statement strike home to our hearts with stark and daring force. That is why we like the title of the book which declares unequivocally that Christians are *Born Crucified*. Yet it is not so incredible when we remember that that same Spirit by which Christ offered himself to God on our behalf (Heb. 9:14) brings us to new birth and indwells our heart. The eternal Spirit of God is not limited by time and space.

Having established that we died in him, Paul goes on in Romans 6:9,10 to emphasise the finality of Christ's death. 'Christ being raised from the dead' — an immortal Man — 'dies no more': 'death has no more dominion over him. For in that he died, he died to sin, once and for all'. 'Likewise ye', says the Apostle (v. 11 A.V.); for if Christ died to sin once and for all, then we also died to sin once and for all, being united to him as those who are for ever dead to sin. Christ has given us from the beginning — since it happened before we were born — a finished work. His work is therefore complete before we receive it, and when we receive it by the Spirit it is a fully accomplished fact.

This takes some believing. If we think we have taken it in our stride and know it all, it may be that the grandeur and wonder of it has not yet struck us. But it must be believed with the whole heart and mind before it can profit us one whit. Many children of God possessing this wonderful finished work do not know it, save in the vaguest and most impracticable sense. It must be known and believed if it is to change our lives.

Is it hard to believe? Look at the word 'count', or 'reckon' in the crucial eleventh verse of Romans 6. It belongs properly to the sphere of the accountant and book-keeper, and means that we are to take stock of what we have. We are therefore to say to ourselves a thousand times a day, 'I am dead indeed to the reign of sin. I have been born into, and am now in, a perfect state of absolute and final death to the reign of sin'.

Do you find this easy to believe? Of course not, for at this point doubts and questionings crowd the mind thick and fast. We argue, 'But I am not dead indeed to sin, for I feel the motions of sin in my members. I sin every day. It cannot be true that I am dead to sin'. Well, it is God's Word against ours. But this argument is a side-track, a satanic side-track, strange as it may seem, to blind us to the spiritual and eternal fact which resides in our breast by the indwelling Holy Spirit. For we cannot have any other Christ within us than that eternal One who came to die our death that he might give himself to us, a blessed gift which we could not acquire of ourselves. Our doubts and fears, with all their thoughts, feelings and experiences, must therefore bow to the Word of God and to the Spirit's witness within our hearts and be silent and believe. Of course, if we come to the conclusion that we are not children of God, that is a different matter, and nothing here stated will then be true of us. In that event we must come to God in repentance, and to Christ in faith (Rev. 3:20), and be converted. But if we know that we are born of God, we must accept that we are born crucified. We are no longer 'slaves to sin' (Rom. 6:6). It no longer rules our lives.

At this point the transcendant finality of it all may stumble us, so that we cannot believe with child-like minds. May we not argue it out? Why, yes. The truth has nothing to fear from the most formidable attack of reasoned incredulity. Think away.

Can our salvation be perfect before it is well begun? The answer is simple. Yes, by virtue of the perfection of the gift that God has given us. We begin perfect in the sense that God has from the beginning done a perfect work in us. But we are not perfect. No, but only a power which is perfect could hope to bring us to perfection. Does not the seed contain within itself the germ of the flower and the fruit? We work from inherent perfection to out-wrought perfection. We do not deny the process of sanctification, but the process is but a drawing upon the resources imparted in the crisis, the new birth. The working out takes time, it may take a lifetime (Phil. 2:12, 13), but the work is from perfection to perfection, from faith to faith, and from glory to glory.

This we must believe before we can begin to grow. The problem of frantic sectarians is often that they refuse to see that the process of sanctification is not something to be wrought into the believer, but to be wrought out. In the new birth we receive *all* that God has to give us, even unto glory (Col. 1:27b). 'What we will be has not yet been made known' (1 John 3:2). Let us learn humbly and gratefully to draw upon this 'all' for everything. We are therefore not dying, but have already died. The process is not *to* death, but *from* death *to* mortification, from inward fact through working faith to outward reality.

Can your heart still not rest in humble and grateful acceptance of this mighty blessing? Do not be surprised; for all the powers of hell will resist your attempts to stand upon Romans 6:11. Every thought and feeling will rise to shout you down as the rankest hypocrite for saying you have indeed died to sin while the motions of sin are still present in your members. We must ignore them all, for 'God is greater than our hearts, and he knows all things' (1 John 3:20). What we ask ourselves is: Lord, are you there? And when he answers, 'Yes' by the inward witness of his Spirit (1 John 5:10), let us acknowledge that we are united to him by eternal and indissoluble bonds and are dead indeed unto sin. Let us believe with all our hearts.

But a voice from beneath says, 'It is one thing to believe it. A man can believe anything if he tries hard enough: but it may not be true. Try putting it into practice and find out if you are really dead to sin'. This sounds reasonable, but is really devilish, and we are not to listen to the devil even when he sounds reasonable. Can we doubt the mischief he intends? Is his name not deceiver? And is he not obliged to deceive to conceal his vile intents? Never mind his taunts.

Nor should we be over-worried about practice at this stage, for if we accept the enemy's challenge and try to 'die to sin' and fail by a hairsbreadth, Satan will laugh in our face and ridicule the whole idea. We are not ready yet to be concerned with practice: we are still engaged in the war to establish faith upon facts. Our chief concern is to know what sort of Jesus dwells in our hearts.

When we are utterly convinced against the apparent evidence of our fluctuating feelings, and against the fiery darts of the wicked one, that we are dead indeed to sin, then is time enough to begin to put faith to the test and prove the mighty power of Christ's death within us; for faith, which then grasps fact, taps power. For if Christ crucified is within us, this means he is there *with all the power of his death*. Paul in 2 Corinthians 4:12 says, 'Death works'. Is it not natural, then, to draw upon what is there? We therefore conclude with Paul in Galatians 2:20 that we 'have been crucified with Christ', and in Colossians 3:3 that we 'are dead'.

But the devil is not done yet. If he cannot shake our faith, he will go to the other extreme (he is fond of extremes). Now, shrewdly acquiescing in what we believe, he will try to draw us away into working it out in our own strength. We must therefore be sure that we are really drawing upon Christ by faith, and not trying to work it up on our own. This does not mean that we sit back and let Christ work within us as an independent Worker. He won't. We have our part to play, which may involve moral sweat, toil, and tears; but always on the understanding that we are drawing on his resources and not working on our own. To co-operate with him does not mean to dispense with him, as if he gave us a push and then left us to ourselves. What makes a motor car go when the driver operates the levers? It is its inherent power, not the man. He sits, almost idly, and makes a few easy, although all-important movements; but he knows that it is not his power which makes the vehicle go, but its own power. It is by works of faith through grace only that we work out our own salvation.

This brings us to Romans 6:12, 13 where we see how perfectly the Scriptures provide knowledge leading to faith and practice. We are not to 'Let sin reign in your mortal body'. This command is addressed to us, but only on the ground of what we have received. It is for lack of strict training in the facts of Scripture that men's faith and feelings go awry. Let us know better, and smash the arrogance of our unbelief by the hammer of God's Word. This is his power to us.

But some will ask: How do we do this? If Christ has done all, what is left for us to do? Well, we must believe, for one thing; but much more. He has broken sin's dominion in his finished work, and while there is nothing left for us to do in that respect, it is only when we 'count' on it that we are ready to do our part, namely that of mortifying what Christ crucified. 'Ah', you say, 'so we mortify'. We do it after all! You must not say that, in view of Christ's mighty work. He has slain, we must mortify (Rom. 8:13). Do you think this is playing with words? Believe it and try it: there is no other way to prove its truth and power. We are to 'count', and let not sin reign, and as we do, the risen life of Christ takes possession of us and his mighty negative of death leads to his glorious positive of life.

There is one further suggestion. What of the dominion of sin? It is slain, but is it rooted out? Yes; but the dregs remain, otherwise salvation would be automatic and would leave no room for the exercise of faith, and heaven would be populated with infants. The remnants of corruption are still there (Rom. 7:14b), but Christ gives us power to keep them in the place of death (Col. 3:5) until they are cast out for ever. If we prove unfaithful to what Christ has made us and let these dregs manifest themselves, we must suffer the consequences. Some people, on account of constant struggling and frequent defeats, have concluded that these remnants are as strong as the new nature, and therefore see no hope in their lives of anything better than a perpetual 'tit-for-tat' of indecisive conflict. This is not so. We may modify the words of John and say, 'Greater is Christ within me than the remnants of sin within me' (1 John 4:4).

Paul also has something to say about this in Romans chapters 5 and 7. Three times in chapter 5, verses 15, 17, 20, he says that Christ is 'much more' than Adam; and in chapter 7, verses 17 and 20, he indicates that a new Christian 'I' has taken the place of the old man. Before Christ came, sin was the householder or owner-occupier: now that Christ has come, sin is dispossessed, and the remnants of corruption remain on sufferance until death parts us for ever from their presence. 'I' am now a Christ-one, committed to live the Christian life, and no longer defer to the Adamic influence. We must accept the fact of the presence of the flesh (Rom. 7:25c), but must refuse its influence in our lives as a power cancelled by Christ's death; and we must regard that potential for evil as an unwelcome residue which we are to mortify by faith in Christ's death, and keep it near the fringe of our lives until we are finally separated from it at death.

Here again, faith must take hold of fact. Do we really believe that Christ within is greater than the presence of sin within? Then let our faith take hold of the fact, even resisting the sin of unbelief to 'blood'. Then we will experience the power of Christ's salvation, not only *from* sin, but for holiness. To this end, we yield to God the new Christian life, whose dregs must be kept down continually because God has no use for them; for who can feed the life of Christ in our soul and fit it for his purposes but God himself who made it? (See Appendix I, p 63).

4

The Third Dimension of the Cross

The Defeat of Satan

When the sin-nature is effectually dealt with and the new Christ-life yielded to God (Rom. 6:3-13), it might be assumed that Paul's next step in Romans would be to unfold the riches of the Spirit-filled life. Not so: there is a chapter-and-a-half yet on the subject of sin, before we read of the Spirit-filled life in chapter 8. Why? What remains to be said, about sin, after it has been destroyed? If we read Romans 6:14 — 7:25 we shall see Paul's continuing preoccupation with sin. Note that *sin is characterised in increasingly personal terms*. In 6:14 it is dominion; from 6:16-23 it is a tyrannical master, a slave-driver; in 7:8 and 7:11 it is an unscrupulous and wily opportunist standing ready to use what is good (the Law) for its own evil purposes; in 7:13, 17, 20, 23 it is a deadly enemy warring against the new man in Christ.

What is this baneful power which Paul cries so

desperately to be delivered from? Surely it is more than the power of inbred sin? It is: it is the devil, lurking behind the remnants of corruption and using them to cloak his presence and working. He is the third dimension of evil which Christ dealt with on the Cross. Our present task is to expose him as deceiver.

'A man sowed good seed in his field; but while men were sleeping, his enemy came and sowed weeds among the wheat . . . And the servants of the householder came and said to him, "Sir, did you not sow good seed in your field? How then has it weeds?" He said to them, "An enemy has done this" ' (Matt. 13:24-28 RSV) *Satan is essentially a deceiver.* Our Lord declared that he was not only a liar, but the father of lies. And he needs to be; for his person and works are so vile that no one would be attracted to him in his own hideous guise. He must needs deceive; and his present deception conceals from sincere but guileless Christians that he is there and at work at all. He does his best (or worst) work in the dark.

To accomplish this he lies so close to the dregs of what we were, that his personal presence is not suspected, and he is consequently able to work upon souls committed to the truth of Romans 6:11 by insidiously stirring up their mortal flesh and (as soon as he has done so) accusing them of sin. We cannot know too much about his wiles. Paul declared that the Christians of his day were 'not ignorant of his devices'. But, today, some professing Christians do not believe in the devil's existence at all, and most Christians have only the haziest notion of his being, location, and working. Some even think it impious and cowardly of us to blame Satan at all for their sin.

It is too easy, admittedly, to blame the devil for our sin; but we are considering those who are free from the reign of sin, and who are taking their stand resolutely against its remaining corruption. For it is to the godly soul, or to him who would be godly, that Satan comes — Job, for example (see Job 1 and 2).

The devil knows that a soul justified by faith in Christ

is lost to him for ever. But he can still work much ill in our life, hindering growth in grace and interfering with training for Christian warfare. And this Satan does by instituting a new campaign of temptation and accusation, which consists of injecting new depths of evil thoughts into the mind, to cast down the godly soul utterly, and make him fear that the truth declared in Romans 6 does not work. This leads to despair, which appears to be Paul's own remembered condition in Romans chapter 7 after Romans 6. That is why he cries out in mortal agony for deliverance from this new, greater, and more virulent 'sin'. But it is not sin, as such, but Satan, hiding in the folds of the fallen nature; who must be dealt with, personally and specifically, before the soul can be delivered from this new and terrible bondage.

Yes, but do we realise the supreme importance of this doctrine of Satan in the biblical unfolding of the meaning of the Cross? The first promise of the Saviour in Genesis 3:15 speaks of deliverance, not from sins, nor from inbred sin, but from Satan, when the seed of the woman shall bruise the serpent's head. This explains the true nature of the conflict between good and evil as all-out war between God and the devil, the battleground being the life of man. Paul confirms this in the climax of the epistle to the Ephesians when he declares in 6:12 that our wrestling is not with flesh and blood (whether our own or that of others), but with spiritual foes still dwelling in the heavenly places which they have defiled. This is made even plainer by our Lord who, when Peter remonstrated with him concerning the prospect of his coming death, turned and addressed his beloved Peter as 'Satan': he saw the devil lurking in Peter's personality.

Does this not set the Christian's after-consecration struggles in a new light? Or do we still think it is too easy to blame the devil? Apparently, for some consecrated Christians prefer, piously and heroically, to blame themselves alone. How wrong and unhealthy! What a shame to turn our gracious Saviour into a policeman. How many are there who crack the legal whip before young Christians and spread the injurious heresy that God is a petty tyrant and slave-driver? What a monstrous travesty of the truth this is! Who is it, then, that Christians are dragooned into worshipping as a superthrasher of saints, with such devastating results? It is the devil, that dread 'angel of light', the accuser of the brethren, 'who accuses them before God day and night.' (Rev. 12:10).

This insight is far too little known. But it is not novel. It is at least as old as *Pilgrim's Progress!* Wrote John Bunyan:

> One thing I would not let slip. I took notice that now poor Christian was so confounded, that he did not know his own voice: and thus I perceived it. Just when he was come over against the mouth of the burning pit, one of the wicked ones got behind him, and stepped up softly to him, and, whisperingly, suggested many grievous blasphemies to him, which he verily thought had proceeded from his own mind. This put Christian more to it than anything that he had met with before, even to think that he should now blaspheme him that he loved so much before. Yet if he could have helped it, he would not have done it; but he had not the discretion either to stop his ears, nor to know from whence these blasphemies came. (See Appendix II, p 63)

But how are we to know when Satan is working in our thoughts? Surely the answer lies on the surface of Bunyan's passage. Christian knew that these were not his own thoughts, certainly not the thoughts of his regenerate heart. After all, he, the regenerate one, was the real man, not fallen Adam. This, doubtless, Bunyan learned from the two illuminating verses in Romans 7 (17, 20), where the Apostle distinguishes between the one voice and the other speaking within him. This is good enough for us. We know that all that is not congruous with the holy law of Christ belongs the the other world, whether of sin or of Satan. Tracing it to its source and author, we ought always to refuse it, even when it subtly tries to mingle itself with what is pure, and gives us certain emotions which we normally associate with the truth. We must not put trust in our feelings. Only emotions which accompany the contemplation of the pure truth of God are to be trusted, and these, not of themselves, but only when accompanied with the truth that gives them rise.

But how are we to deal with this element in our lives if it is not only sinful but demonic? Is the thought that we are moved by perverse and malign spiritual intelligencies not unnerving? Not if we know the truth. Satan and all his crew have been dealt with. Jesus, who died to take away our sins and to overthrow sin, also died to defeat Satan and his powers, for us. For us! Just as we have wrestled with the paradox which says that we are dead to sin but must yet keep down the remaining dross, so we must now wrestle with the further paradox that Christ has finally defeated Satan for us on the Cross, but we must make his victory our own by battling in his strength.

Take the fact of Christ's victory over the ultimate person of evil, the devil. Hebrews 2:14,15 bluntly states that 'since the children share in flesh and blood, he himself likewise partook of the same nature, that through death he might destroy [bring to nought] him who has the power of death, that is, the devil, and deliver all those who through fear of death were subject to lifelong bondage.' (RSV) And 1 John 3:8 is plain: 'The reason the Son of God appeared was to destroy the devil's work. Colossians 2:15 says that Christ stripped, or disarmed 'the principalities and powers and made a public example of them, triumphing over them in it [the Cross]', or 'in him' [Christ].

What do these Scriptures mean? That Christ took upon himself the very human nature in which Adam succumbed to Satan's power, and gained victory over the foe in it for Adam. John H. Newman's hymn helps greatly:

> *O loving wisdom of our God!*
> *When all was sin and shame,*
> *A second Adam to the fight*
> *And to the rescue came.*
>
> *O wisest love! that flesh and blood,*
> *Which did in Adam fail,*
> *Should strive afresh against the foe,*
> *Should strive and should prevail . . .*
>
> *O generous love! that he who smote*
> *In Man, for man, the foe,*
> *The double agony in Man,*
> *For man, should undergo.*

Easter hymns love to trumpet forth the clarion note of Christ's victory over the enemy, but Newman's hymn goes further than many in declaring that the victory was *for man*, that is, *for us*.

To understand what this means we must remember that Christ the eternal Son of God and Co-Creator with the Father had no need of personal victory over the devil: he was not in his power. Rather, the devil was a creature of the three-in-one God, whom he could destroy in a moment. It is unthinkable that Christ should need to inhabit a human body to gain victory over the devil for himself. It is Christ who holds all things together in his hands (Col. 1:17; Heb. 1:2, 3). He won the victory for us: that was the lengths to which his love went to retrieve our ruin. Hence Paul cries out in the great resurrection chapter, 'Thanks be to God. He gives us the victory through our Lord Jesus Christ.' (1 Cor. 15:57).

He gives us the victory! The Easter hymns are largely

content to shout Christ's own victory, as if he won it for himself, and not for us. It was for us, and its great purpose begins to ʰe realised only when we see it, and enter into its fruits, as did the saints in Revelation 12:11.

That whole passage describing God's victory in Christ over Satan, ought to be studied (Rev. 12:7-12). Its climax declares that our brethren, who are accused day and night by Satan, overcame him through the blood of the Lamb, and through the word of their witness (to that fact), which witness they maintained, not loving their lives even to martyrdom. Think what this means: *Men overcame Satan*, through Christ's victory over him. Therefore, *we may overcome him, too.* Is it not tremendous that mere sinners, formerly under absolute bondage to God's implacable enemy, may now, by trusting in Jesus' death, overcome him, because Jesus died to procure that victory for them?

This is why James challenges us: 'Resist the devil, and he will flee from you' (Jas. 4:7). Peter also warns us that our 'enemy the devil prowls around like a roaring lion looking for someone to devour'; adding, 'Resist him, standing firm in the faith.' (1 Pet. 5:8,9) But let Jesus have the last word: 'No one can enter a strong man's house, and carry off his possessions [the enslaved souls of men, including believers still partly in his power], unless he first ties up the strong man. Then he can rob his house.' (Mark 3:27).

Christ has given us the power to bind the strong man, the devil, and spoil his goods, and this includes the freeing of our souls, and the souls of others, progressively from his thrall. But first we must let the facts of Christ's power sink deep into our minds until faith rises to take hold of them. Then faith will take hold of the enemy where his influence lives, and shake him until he flees for his life.

The victory Christ gained for us over the enemy is full and final, but we must, none the less, battle our way into it, inch by inch, through his power. We must, therefore, lay our plans in full Bible knowledge. If we do, we shall soon see three clearly discernible stages in the development of the Christian life, from childhood to soldierhood.

1. A believer is born of Christ as a babe, and is spiritually in need of milk food because he cannot stand strong meat (1 Cor. 3:1-3; Heb. 5:12-14; 1 Pet. 2:2). Infants cannot serve.

2. A true babe in Christ, if nourished in God's Word, will grow and become fit for the service of God. (There were forty hidden years in Moses' life, thirty in our Lord's, and ten in Paul's after his conversion.) He will then serve according to his calling and gifts.

3. A servant cannot fight until he knows the enemy, within and without, and has been trained in the use of Christian armour, weapons, and strategy: then he becomes a soldier. This is the theme of our next chapter.

5

The Training of a Christian Soldier

As there are three stages in the development of the Christian life from childhood through servanthood to soldierhood, so there are three stages in his training as a Christian soldier. They are:

1. Strategic Retreat.
2. Unyielding Defence.
3. All-out Attack.

We must learn *how*, *when*, and *where* to *run for shelter* from overwhelming danger; *stand for resolute defence*; and *advance to confident attack*.

1. Strategic Retreat

It may seem contradictory to what we have stated concerning victory in Christ, immediately to counsel young soldiers to run from the enemy; but it is necessary. Discretion is often the better part of valour, especially when God lets Satan loose upon us for our training. He is, of course, never really loose: God simply lengthens his chain, and allows him scope to try us. But it is a frightening experience to face his snarling advance, and at first we may want to turn and flee, not into Christ, but away from the whole terrifying business of being a Christian at all. Many have tried to do so and have striven to maintain an uneasy compromise between Christ and the devil and heaven and hell, but without success. Besides, God's Word strictly and sternly forbids us to fear Satan. How many 'Fear nots' are there in the Bible? Yet part of our training is to know the enemy, and before we have the unspeakable thrill of putting him to flight, we must learn what a terrible foe he is. As we learn we will realise that it is important to know where to run for shelter, for there are days of Satan's power (see Luke 22: 53b) when even the strongest is well-advised to run to Christ for safety. The Scriptures teach this.

David in his Song of Deliverance from his enemies says: 'The Lord is my rock, my fortress, and my deliverer; my God is my rock; in whom I take refuge, my shield, and the horn of my salvation. He is my stronghold, my refuge and my saviour — from violent men you save me' (2 Sam. 22:2; see also Ps. 18:2). The same great soldier says again: 'Hear my cry, O God; listen to my prayer. From the ends of the earth I call to you, I call as my heart grows faint; lead me to the rock that is higher than I. For you have been my refuge, a strong tower against the foe. I long to dwell in your tent for ever, and take refuge in the shelter of your wings (Ps. 61:1-4). And the mighty general's son Solomon: 'The name of the Lord is a strong tower: the righteous run to it, and are safe (Prov. 18:10).

Much is said about the increasing tendency to escape the pressures of modern life, and some escapes, like those into drugs or suicide, are bad. But escape is sometimes necessary. No man is able to cope with the evil in the world unaided. But the Christian is not unaided. He has Christ for his shelter, and must learn, especially in the evil day (Eph. 6:13), to beat an ordered retreat from him and hide in the Rock of Ages until Satan's fury is past (see Ps. 57:1).

We need to be forewarned of Satan's attacks when we enter the training school for spiritual warfare, for they usually come suddenly, and from the least expected quarter. It may be an inward attack, or it may come from without, as a bolt from the blue, to demoralise us before we know where we are. It is a real enemy we are fighting, who will stop at nothing to knock us out of the fight before we are in it.

Many Christians who accept this kind of teaching in general without personal knowledge of the devil's malevolence, and who are therefore innocently sceptical of it, are alarmed when he cuts across their path, or makes them fall flat on their faces on the threshold of a great campaign. Consequently, they reel and wonder what has hit them. But we must not panic, nor become morbidly preoccupied with dread of Satan, but set a serious watch, and reckon that without looking for trouble, he will attack.

2. Unyielding Defence

It is wonderful to run into Christ in the evil hour and, with the enemy roaring all around, know that he is powerless to touch us. Only then, when we have learned in practice what we know in theory, do we realise that *Jesus is stronger than Satan.* With this new confidence in our Saviour's power we are ready for the next stage in our training, and we graduate to a higher class in the Captain's school. There is a paradox here; for we must always run into Christ in danger, since we are ourselves defenceless souls. Yet God is not only our refuge, but our strength. Sheltered in him and made aware of the armour he provides, we are soon encouraged to don its several pieces and think about facing the foe. When Satan next attacks, instead of cowering in the corners of our shelter, we dare to stand forth and resist him bravely. Hebrews 2:14, 1 John 3:8, and Colossians 2:15 have already afforded us typical ground for believing in Christ's victory: now we begin to accept the fact that the power of Christ to shelter us from the devil may also fortify us in confronting him.

But before we go to the battlefield, we need to be reassured that Christ's victory will be personally available to us. To believe this calls for a tremendous effort of faith, and we must learn to grapple to our hearts such words as 'gives us' in 1 Corinthians 15:57 and 'they overcame him' in Revelation 12:11, to know that his victory is ours. This is not easy, even if we have the example of the heroes of faith in Hebrews 11. However many saints have trusted in God's power and found it effectual, this is *our* first attempt in a new dimension. It is as if not only we, but Christ also, were being tested anew. In fact, it demands a trust in Christ's deed and Word which in the critical event is nothing less than the dying of a death to all defeatist, emotional rationalisations that are likely to assail us in the conflict. This is simply a matter of following Christ into that death by which he gained his victory. We gain ours likewise, by following where he first victoriously led. If it does not work with us, then not only do we fail, but he fails also, for his Word is proved ineffectual. God cannot take that risk, and is as much concerned that his power works with us as with his Son; for it is wrought for his Son in his death, that it might work for us in ours. 'For us' is our fortification, and thus fortified, we go forward confidently to face the foe. And we had better, as Jeremiah the timidest of prophets found when he was commanded to face the whole evil might of decadent Jewry.

Jeremiah sought to excuse himself to the Lord because, he said, he was a child and could not speak (Jer. 1:6). But

God said, 'Now, I have put my words in your mouth.' (v.9), 'Do not be afraid of them; for I am with you and will rescue you' (v. 8) And, lest he falter, God added, 'Get yourself ready! Stand up and say to them whatever I command you. Do not be terrified by them or I will terrify you before them. Today I have made you a fortified city, an iron pillar, and a bronze wall against the whole land . . . They will fight against you but will not overcome you for I am with you and will rescue you' (vv.17-19).

Thus exposed to the blasts of the enemy, there is no alternative to naked faith in the Word of the Lord, no alternative but complete demoralisation, and defeat!

Turn to David again. Here is a hardy word of encouragement for such a time, and from a surprising place — the Shepherd Psalm. The writer is in the valley of the shadow of death, not knowing, apart from their occasional growls, where the wild beasts lurk amongst the surrounding crags; and he is calmly sitting down to a sumptuous meal while his person is groomed, even to the anointing of his head (Ps. 23:4,5)! Could we enjoy a feast if a roaring lion were about to leap upon us?

But the fullest and most helpful passage on the exploit is in Ephesians 6:10-18. Following the introduction (10-13), note the four 'stands', in 11, 13 (twice), and 14. It is easy to say 'Stand', but when all the demons of hell are let loose it is not easy to stand, let alone sit and indulge ourselves. But in Christ we do not stand defenceless and exposed to the enemy's onslaughts, but are provided with suitable dress for the battle. To this we now turn.

(i) The Belt of Truth

the first item of defensive armour is the belt of truth. The Scriptures have much to say about 'girding the loins'. They bid us gather ourselves together for action as soldiers gird themselves for battle. The girdle or belt applied to truth reminds us that only the truth can prevail in the war against falsehood.

> *Fain would we join the blest array,*
>   *And follow in the might*
> *Of him, the Faithful and the True,*
>   *In raiment clean and white.*
> *Yet who can fight for truth and God,*
>   *Enthralled by lies and sin?*
> *He who would wage such war on earth*
>   *Must first be true within.*
>
> (Thomas Hughes)

The Apostle is probably referring both to the whole body of biblical truth, and to particular truths declaring God's power and victory over the forces of evil. What are these? They concern the nature of God and the devil and the different dimensions of their activities:

1. God the Father is the uncreated and unbegotten One, whereas Satan is a creature gone wrong, whom God could destroy in a moment if he chose.

2. Christ the eternal Son, the only-begotten of the Father, has gained final victory over Satan, as Newman says, 'in Man for man' (see p. 00 22). See also Hebrews 2:14; 1 John 3:8; Colossians 2: 15; Revelation 12:7-11.

3. God the eternal Spirit, following Pentecost, brings the efficacies of Christ's victorious death to the hearts and lives of those who believe in him.

If in face of the enemy's attacks we bind these truths to us and refuse to let them be torn from us, we will repulse the enemy, and rejoice to see him driven defeated from the field.

(ii) The Breastplate of Righteousness

But Satan is not done with us by any means, and we must be prepared for further attacks. We must put on the breastplate of righteousness, to withstand his attack both upon our standing and our state in Christ, for he will try to deny both our imputed and our imparted righteousness. The breastplate particularly guards the heart, and it is in the heart that we must believe that Christ is our righteousness (see Rom. 10:10; Jer. 23:6; and 1 Cor. 1:30). This is our standing.

But it is perhaps especially in respect of our moral state, or state of actual righteousness, that we are assailed by Satan. We shall not be *perfect* while we are in this mortal body, but we can be *blameless*.

It is only as we preserve moral integrity before God by the Spirit's aid that, as to basic virtues of honesty, purity, humility and charity, we can withstand the enemy's assaults.

At this stage we may expect massive attacks upon basic virtues. We should not be surprised even although we are appalled, at some of the impure and dishonest thoughts that he causes to pass through our minds. These are not ordinary temptations of the flesh, although they come through the flesh. They come from the enemy himself. Further, their sudden coming is generally related to some opportunity about to present itself for fruitful witness or service. The fact that Satan is trying something on in relation to the (possibly) immediate future should encourage us to resist his emotional enticements. It is far more exciting to resist a sudden pleasurable sensation or tempting thought and subsequently discover where the devil was trying to gain an advantage over us, than to yield to it without a struggle!

This is a common attack on young servants of God, as is plain from Paul's words to Timothy: 'I give you this instruction in keeping with the prophecies once made about you, so that by following them you may fight the good fight, holding on to faith and a good conscience. Some have rejected these and so have shipwrecked their faith' (1 Tim.1:18-19). Again, a leader 'must not be a recent convert, or he may become conceited and fall under the same judgment as the devil' (1 Tim.3:6-7). Peter adds, 'as aliens and strangers in the world . . . abstain from sinful desires, which war against your soul' (1 Pet.2:11). Again, says Paul, 'Do not give the devil a foothold' (Eph.4:27).

We must guard our inward moral integrity as our life; for, if we fail here, we fail utterly. Yet if we begin to see how cunningly occasional, or tactically planned these temptations are, we shall soon be wise, not only to them, but to him (Satan).

(iii) The Gospel of Peace

We are taking the pieces of defensive armour in Ephesians 6 in progressive and culminating sequence, although some think this goes beyond the scriptural warrant. Perhaps; but that there is a progession is plain from the fact that the defensive comes before the offensive; the shield, *etc.* before the·sword of the Spirit and the weapon of all-prayer. We shall maintain this progression, but those who reject it need not reject the truth associated with it: we are not trying to impose an arbitrary pattern of diabolical attacks upon the spiritual progress of every soul — even a little knowledge of human psychology shows how foolish that would be.

The attack upon our personal, moral integrity is a serious one, and the devil, successfully repulsed, may now retire to devise new and more cunning tactics against us. If he cannot shake our moral convictions or undermine our moral character, he has other weapons in his diabolical armoury, and will doubtless try more powerful means to move us, in the hope that he may shatter our peace of mind.

He may now assail us with a sense of restless foreboding, and with irrational fears, until we seriously doubt God, ourselves, and, in fact, everything that is good. All joy goes out of life, nothing seems to matter, a vague, gnawing, cynical dread underlies all we formerly thought secure; the whole world begins to heave and turn like an ocean giant plunging to its doom. These are not ordinary feelings of unhappiness; indeed, they can be so enveloping and total that it is hard to believe they are real. But they are only too real — yet they seem so unlikely that it is impossible to talk about them; people would not understand.

Not many understand, although many suffer. But God who permits them understands, and he has a word, several words, for them. Here is one, whose bedrock dependability has been proved for ages by those in dire need: 'You will keep in perfect peace, him whose mind is steadfast, because he trusts in you. Trust in the Lord forever, for the Lord, the Lord is the rock eternal' (Is.26:3,4). This is not biblical jargon with meaning only for the initiated, but an anchor of truth for all to hold on to when the whole world seems to be giving way.

Here is another word, this time from Paul: 'Do not be anxious about anything; but in everything by prayer and petition, with thanksgiving, present your request to God. And the peace of God, which transcends all understanding, will guard your hearts and minds in Christ Jesus' (Phil. 4:6,7). And again, 'And over all these virtues put on love, which binds them all together in perfect unity. Let the peace of Christ rule [preside] in your hearts' (Col. 3:14, 15).

With Scriptures such as these — and it is not the number of them but the penetration of their truth that counts — the sorely tried soldier, his feet well shod with the good news of God's care and provision, can take his stance and hold his ground against the most hellish attack. This is especially true, since the Father is watching that he may not be tempted beyond what he is able to bear (1 Cor. 10:13). After all, it is not only our faith in Christ which daunts Satan, but the watchful eye of the Almighty. He will not suffer us to be overwhelmed by him. It is well to remember that when we are tried, and tempted to resign ourselves to the darkness of defeat, the enemy also may be almost played out. If we can hold on, he will collapse and let go. He must and will, because we are trusting in him who has vanquished him, once and for all. Jesus' own heart-rending cry was just before the end. What devilish pressure was laid upon him we do not know, but it was 'for the joy that was set before him' that 'he endured' (Heb. 12:2). He had all to gain or all to lose, and he emerged triumphant in victorious death and resurrection. So shall we, if we endure, and be ready to fight another day, with strengthened faith.

(iv) The Shield of Faith

The enemy will at this point need to regain his breath. He is not invincible, and more easily shaken by those in Christ than we realise. But while he calls an infernal conference (*cf.* C. S. Lewis' *Screwtape Letters*) and desperately tries to plan new and more deadly attacks, we may list, not proudly, but humbly and thankfully, the growing tale of our victories — all to Christ's glory. Yet these will not suffice for his next attack: we must also set ourselves to test our defences, and seek to found our faith more securely on the Rock of Ages, so that we may stand together with Christ against the further demoralising attacks the enemy is about to launch. We need a huge shield of faith to quench all the fire-tipped darts which he is about to hurl at us from all directions, in an all-out blitz.

But what does the imagery of the fire-tipped dart represent in experience? A series of sudden, totally unexpected attacks, usually very different from one another, aimed at shaking our faith in God, his revealed

Word and will to his children, and our judgment, obedience and sincerity.

For example, a young servant of God awaiting news of an examination is seized with a feeling of vile and impure hands laid upon her, and the feeling persists and grows until she is well-nigh demented. Exhorted to resist in faith and believe for success (having done all she could to merit it) she does so, and when the good news about the examination comes through, the attack ends as suddenly as it began.

Another example: a young missionary, his leave long overdue, looks forward eagerly to the voyage home to relieve the almost unbearable strain of a trying tour of service. The days before embarkation are spent in a hospitable home where the children are suffering from an exceedingly infectious disease. On the night of the embarkation the awful though strikes him that he is a carrier of the disease and dare not go on board. There were no symptoms, nothing to ground the obsessing fear upon but the overpowering thought, confronting him like a barrier at the gangway. Almost mad with tension, he nevertheless resists the thought, and the next day, with trepidation, goes on board.

The first few days on ship were hell to his tortured mind: he avoided every one, especially the children, as if he were a leper. No symptoms appeared, however, and the gripping fear began to relax, and the remainder of the voyage was pleasant, beneficial, and fruitful in spiritual profit to others. Only those who have experienced this kind of thing can appreciate the inward agony.

Here is another story of a tried and trusted servant of God. It has two parts, one comparatively trivial, the other more serious, illustrating the varied stratagems of the enemy. A young man intent on serving God had begun to prepare for Christian service. He had a happy nature with a normally healthy outlook on life, but had become increasingly obsessed with the morbid suspicion that to be too happy was sinful. One day he saw something he wanted in a shop window and went in to buy it. The shopkeeper appeared, and instantly the inward tyrant hissed, 'You cannot have it: it is sin!' Dumbfounded at the violence of the warning, he fled from the shop leaving the astonished shopkeeper gaping.

The other part of the story concerns a university grant. Financial assistance was not easily come by then, and the young man's parents were not able to finance his education. But he was assured he would receive a grant, and was about to sign the application form when the sinister voice spat out, 'You cannot do it, it is sin!' Several years of financial aid were thereby unsigned away, leading to years of hardship.

This form of attack came with increasing frequency and ferocity until a sane and balanced young man became almost demented, not only by its unpredictableness, but by the horrid discovery that the 'God' he had believed to be so loving was really a monster. (Compare the experience of Job, for example, in chapters 9 and 10.)

It is all very well to say that Satan's bluff should have been called earlier; but he is a spirit, and when he comes in this way, and young Christians have no teaching on the workings of evil spirits, the very force of the attacks is frighteningly impressive, and his victims are driven to comply in sheer terror, lest they fight against God.

As this form of attack developed increasingly in the young man's life, his early ministry was periodically overwhelmed by a pall of spiritual darkness completely enshrouding his soul. He had to preach the Word even while the black conviction gripped him that he himself was lost, a Christless soul; and others were converted through his preaching even while this was his own experience. Eventually, although it took years, the ground comparatively innocently conceded to the enemy was retaken, albeit with painful failures and setbacks, until at last there was full deliverance. The fruits of this man's ministry are now well known, and the reason for Satan's desperate attempts to stop it before it had well nigh started is fully exposed.

It is the suddenness and unexpectedness of the attacks which are alarming, as also the imperious demand that the spirit is to be obeyed instantly without question — and without reason.

How then are we to distinguish between the voice of God and the voice of Satan? We know, of course, that God can give his servants swift guidance, but he never 'blitzes' them. He has no need; for even when he comes suddenly, he is sweetly reasonable and identifies himself by his loving wisdom, and thus we recognise him. Normally he takes his time to tell us something new, and allows his gently growing pressure to convince us that it is indeed our heavenly Father who is speaking. He never dragoons, least of all those who are being trained to be his valued servants. He has a specially tender care and regard for them.

(v) The Helmet of Salvation

This is the last piece of defensive armour — salvation for the head. The attack which it serves to ward off is certainly the devil's worst. Indeed, true children of God, who are not, all of them, old and senile, can be attacked. Evil can assail those who are normally sane, whether they have a predisposition to mental illness or not.

It is too painful and embarrassing to discuss modern examples, but a notable scriptural example illustrates the possibility, that of Israel's first king, Saul. To understand the example fully we must read his life story in 1 Samuel, chapters 10-26, when it will be hard to escape the conclusion that that magnificent specimen of manhood was attacked by the devil, or some demonic spirit or spirits, to his ruin.

But surely the intimate stories of missionaries who have challenged the kingdom of darkness and have paid for their pains, tell of what the wrecker can do to God's soldiers if the head is not protected from his diabolical attacks. Nothing less than the helmet of salvation will save in this situation. The last piece of defensive armour must be a scriptural word defying the total ingenuity and might of the devil himself. Such a word is, 'submit yourselves, then, to God. Resist the devil, and he will flee from you' (Jas. 4:7; also 1 Pet. 5:8, 9).

But the helmet needs to be firmly fitted to protect the whole mind. We must boldly react against the desperate wiles of the devil until he is thoroughly shaken. This is a tremendous thing to do, for it involves nothing less than standing between God and the devil, and daring to declare that we intend to prove in our own mind and body that Jesus is stronger than Satan. Furthermore, that brave attitude must understand that the salvation of the mortal life is at stake, for it has its back to the wall, is faced by an implacable foe, and is fighting for nothing less than survival as a practising Christian. The devil must yield.

Do we ask what will happen if he does not? Well, if we were to draw on the victorious resources of Jesus Christ in the evil day and found that they did not work, we would have proved Christ's claims false, and could trust him no more. But he cannot fail: his integrity depends upon him delivering his people in the 'evil day'. Why, even the survival of the universe, and his own survival, depend upon that! We may be called with the Apostle to be 'exposed to death again and again' (2 Cor. 11:23), but through it all there must be resurrections, either in this world, or, in the case of martyrdoms, in the next. We can be as sure as God that in Christ there is victory for us (1 Cor. 15:57).

3. All-out Attack

We are almost weary of the word 'attack' as applied to the enemy. It will be a change to re-apply it to ourselves in Christ. When the devil, who cannot destroy the servants and soldiers of God, but only render them unfit for service, sees that we have won our spurs, he will withdraw from us for a little. He is not gone for ever, but has retired to plan fresh attacks. But we have learned that in the strength of Christ he can be repulsed. We have gained something of his measure, and the lesson is not lost on us. We are now ready to wield the sword of the Spirit which is the Word of God.

(i) The Sword of the Spirit

We have used the Word of God before in our defence (Eph. 6:14). We are now to learn to hurl it at the enemy as Jesus did in his temptations. How do we do it? Just as he did (Matt. 4:1-11). He took three 'rocks' of holy Scripture (Deut. 8:3; 6:16; 6:13) and flung them at the devil until he departed, beaten. The devil can quote the Scriptures, too, but if we compare Matthew 4:6 with Psalm 91:11-12, we shall see that Satan, like so many, leaves out what does not suit his purpose. He uses the Scriptures to deceive, trap and destroy us if he can: whereas Jesus uses them to destroy what is evil. We see who uses them successfully in the temptation account.

The difference between Jesus' use of the Scriptures, and the devil's use of them is this: Satan tinkers with them and loses their force by leaving out God's promise to keep his people while they walk in His ways. Jesus uses them simply, and, united to the Father and the Spirit speaking in holy Writ, resists him effectually. It is, therefore, identification with the triune God speaking in Scripture which is our strength, not trying to add to or subtract from God's Word (*cf.* Rev. 22:18,19). To prove the power of God in his Word we must stand foursquare upon it with Jesus.

We are now in a realm where we may not only withstand the enemy on our own behalf, but on behalf of others. This is a tremendous thrill, which will be even more obvious when we come to the use of the other offensive weapon, all-prayer. The writer to the Hebrews tells us that, 'The word of God is living and active, sharper than any two-edged sword, piercing to the division of soul and spirit . . . discerning the thoughts and intentions of the heart. And before him (note the unity of God with his Word) no creature is hidden.' (Heb. 4:12,13a RSV).

When we use God's Word in accordance with his will, we have all the consent and power of the Almighty behind us. We therefore take the word of Jesus which commands us to bind the strong man (the poetic figure of binding is not congruous with that of swiping with a sword, but the truths belong together) in order to spoil his goods (the souls of men held in his thrall). We shall find that when we exert ourselves to do this with an energy and devotion at least as keen as we apply to selfish pursuits, lo, people begin to respond to God's Word, perhaps to our great surprise. It is not to be wondered at. The truth is that men's hearts and lives are in fact in bondage to Satan (1 John 5:19) and when his power is broken, they are free to hear and heed God's Word.

This is a great secret; and yet many of us go on in Christian work year by year, dealing with men as if they were normally free agents willing and able to do what we say, or what they themselves will. They are not (Rom. 7:14-20), until God frees them in answer to prevailing prayer.

(ii) All-Prayer

The connection of the sword of the Spirit with prayer is clear. It is not in direct witness, public or private, that the battle for souls is won, but in the closet and prayer room (Matt. 6:6). Far too many who are engaged in Christian service do not appreciate this. They also are blinded by Satan, and we may wonder whether they believe in God at all, except as some rudimentary, vague spirit who sits content with perfunctory religion.

There are two possible meanings of all-prayer: (1) that it includes all forms of prayer; (2) that it means all-out prayer. This seems to be what the Apostle has in mind in Ephesians 6:18. It is *total war*, demanding *total dedication*. The plain truth is that as Christ did not save us short of his death, neither will we save others short of his death in us, whatever that death may be or may mean for us personally.

The most searching word on this is found in 2 Corinthians 4:10-12, where Paul speaks of dying and rising on his own behalf (10, 11), and for others (12). This is the death which defeats Satan. It defeated him fundamentally and finally on the Cross, and it defeats him in our lives and in the lives of others as we stand with the Crucified and Risen One resisting to 'blood' (Heb. 12: 4).

This 'death' in prayer has two effects, which scripture describes as 'fasting' and 'prayer'. 'Fasting' indicates the negative part of it in temporarily denying ourselves the legitimate pleasures of life, whereas 'prayer' indicates the positive part of entering into the intercessory death-throes that bind Satan. Such intercessory death enables God to open men's hearts and minds to receive the Word of Truth with unblinded and unbiased honesty. It also gives utterance to witnesses to the truth (whether speaking in private, or in public), who let the Holy Spirit through from the throne of God to their hearts, and then to the hearts of their hearers, and back again to heaven. The whole sequence and circle of the divine purpose is thus wonderfully threaded through to its completion.

'All-Prayer' is therefore not an 'added extra' to evangelism. It is so vital a part of evangelism that no true evangelism can exist without it (see Eph. 6:19-20).

6

Christian Service and Warfare

It cannot be too clearly stated, or too often repeated, that God has only one Worker, the Holy Spirit. In all we hope to become and do for God we never take over from him.

God will not surrender his sovereignty to his creatures. Indeed, in all our Lord's amazing 'homecoming' to sinful humanity by his incarnate, saving love, he is always careful to make the distinction between God and man. Jesus does not pray or speak to the Father as we do, saying 'our Father', but, 'my Father' (John 20:17. It is only in the Only-Begotten that we are adopted into the Father's family. Even so, we remain creature-sons and daughters, as he ever remains the Creator-Son. This means that our dependence on God's power must be constant and absolute, as Jesus' stark statement shows: 'When you have done everything you were told to do . . . say, 'We are unworthy servants; we have only done our duty' (Lk. 17:10). Whereas Paul declares, 'I can do everything through him who gives me strength' (Phil. 4:13), Jesus says, 'Apart from me you can do nothing' (John 15:5).

There is great danger of the intrusion of the flesh (fallen humanity) into Christian service. It is surely for this reason that in moments of high spiritual strategy God makes indubitably plain that the authority, initiative, and execution of his will remain always and only in his hands.

An illustration of this is provided in Exodus 14 when the Red Sea barred the escape of the Israelites fleeing from the Egyptians. Something had to be done — and quickly! Moses turned to the panic-stricken people and shouted, 'Do not be afraid. Stand firm and you will see the deliverance the Lord will bring you today. The Egyptians you see today, you will never see again. The Lord will fight for you; you need only to be still' (Ex. 14:13-14).

But they did not stand idle. God said, 'Go forward, right down to the shore, and see what I will do.' And they did; for salvation, all of grace, is nevertheless of faith, the gift of God's grace. In this instance, the fact that redemption was all of God was acknowledged later by Moses and Israel when they sang their song of triumph:

'I will sing to the Lord, for he is highly exalted.
   The horse and its rider he has hurled into the sea.
The Lord is my strength and my song; he has become
   my salvation.
He is my God, and I will praise him,
   my father's God, and I will exalt him.
The Lord is a warrior;
   The Lord is his name.' (Ex. 15:1-3)

We find the same emphasis in the story of David. In gratitude for his victories over the enemies of Israel, he desired to build a house for the Lord. God said, 'The Lord himself will build a house for you' (2 Sam. 7-11).

The house David intended, and which Solomon eventually built, was of wood and stone. The house God promised to build for David was his lineage, even to 'great David's greater Son', then to us and all the children of God. That house is *God's* building, although we help to build it and are part of it and shall dwell in it one day. The fine balance of God's working and of our co-operation with him is perfectly expressed in Paul's exhortation: 'Work out your salvation with fear and trembling, for it is God who works in you to will and to act according to his good purpose' (Phil. 2:12, 13).

A God so great in power will not share his honour and glory with us. 'I am the Lord; that is my name! I will not give my glory to another.' (Is. 42:8) 'Therefore if any one is in Christ, he is a new creation; the old has gone, the new has come. All this is from God.' (2 Cor. 5:17, 18a) 'Whether you eat, or drink, or whatever you do, do it all for the glory of God' (1 Cor. 10:31).

God is the only Worker, for all that we do in him is by his power. Those who seek to serve him and fight for him must be morally, intellectually and emotionally convinced that all the glory is his, and that the uncreated God will never share his sole prerogative with his creatures. What he shares are his blessings, and the man in Christ can have his fill of them — certainly more than he seeks.

7

Spiritual Maturity

We have called this book *Towards Spiritual Maturity*, not *Towards Spiritual Victory*. Why? Because spiritual maturity is more than the achievement of victorious service. Certainly, none can serve God without a measure of maturity, as none can fight for him without a measure of understanding of, and training for the realities of spiritual conflict.

We have heard the claim, and have supported it, that the highest divine service on earth is intercession. Is there not a higher? Not higher, but different, which necessarily belongs with fruitful intercession. It is love to Jesus, and enjoyment of God. This is highest worship, highest maturity, and highest service, all in one. It runs side by side with the mighty warfare of intercession and with effective public service for Christ. It stands to reason that we cannot be often at the throne of grace without coming to know the Occupant of the throne. We cannot be much on active service in the interests of his

glory without enjoying the fruits of that co-operation
with him. Indeed, this both precedes all we can say, and
is the sum of it.

> *The love of Jesus, what it is*
> *None but his loved ones know!*

There is a zeal for God (*cf.* Rom. 10:2-4) and for the
honour of his name which may work itself to death in
sacrifice and endurance ('if I surrender my body to the
flames', 1 Cor. 13:3), but whose motive is neither high
enough nor pure enough to gain the Lord's co-operation,
or his commendation. Such was the case with the
Ephesians in Revelation 2:1-7. They had left their first
love, Jesus, and consequently their highest and best was
at least suspect. There is no loyalty, faithfulness,
obedience, endurance, or suffering that can pass the all-
seeing eye of heaven's Majesty except it springs from love
to Jesus.

Let us look further into this in connection with what we
have been saying. We have seen that God hates three
elements in fallen man — his sins, his sin, and the
influence of Satan on him. Having learned from God's
Word of Christ's complete provision against all three,
and that there is nothing and no one to fear beyond these,
we may enter into the infinite and eternal inheritance
which Christ's victory has gained for us, namely that of
the 'peace that passes all understanding'.

'Where sin increased, grace increased all the more'
(Rom. 5:20). There is no doubt about the pleasure we have
in God when we see the real size of the enemy, for all the
evil which God implacably hates we then see to be but
serving his purpose, by evoking responses of divine grace
to deal with it.

We know, of course, that we must not sin that grace
may abound (Rom. 6:1,2). Yet we must nevertheless
rejoice that all the evil and sin which God permits he
purposes to use to his glory. When Simon the Pharisee

inwardly despised Jesus for regarding the woman 'who was a sinner', Jesus replied, 'I tell you, her many sins have been forgiven for she loved much. But he who has been forgiven loves little' (Luke 7:47). The grace of abundant forgiveness of many sins evokes a commensurate love in the forgiven sinner. This turns the so-called problem of evil not only into a mystery solved, but into such a cause of rejoicing and thanksgiving to God as surely makes the vaults of heaven ring and its courts resound with angelic praise.

We have sometimes thought the laughter of God at the attempts of Satan to hurt him must be so hearty and incredulous as to be too much for over-serious Christians to hear! The amazement of heaven at the devil's niggling attempts to do despite to God and his work must be astonishing. No one who knows that God is on the throne and that 'all things work together for good to them that love God' can possibly have a qualm or fear about anything. Things being as they are by the victory of Christ, there remains nothing to preoccupy the heart and mind beyond Jesus.

Let us be sure about this. If we look at Exodus chapters 7 to 9 we shall see that six times Pharaoh hardened his heart (7:13,14; 7:22; 8:15; 19; 32; 9:7), but in 9:12 'the Lord hardened the heart of Pharaoh', which suggests that God ultimately confirmed Pharaoh in his chosen path of sin. But Pharaoh's sin, confirmed by God, does not frustrate the Almighty (see Rom. 9:17,18). The Egyptian king resisted God to his own destruction, and to the destruction of his army.

'In the morning watch the Lord looked down from the pillar of fire and cloud at the Egyptian army and threw it into confusion. He made the wheels of their chariots come off so that they had difficulty driving. And the Egyptians said, "Let's get away from the Israelites! The Lord is fighting for them against Egypt." Then the Lord said to Moses, "Stretch out your hand over the sea so that the waters may flow back over the Egyptians and their

chariots and horsemen." Moses stretched out his hand
over the sea, and at daybreak the sea went back to its
place. The Egyptians were fleeing towards it, and the
Lord swept them into the sea' (Ex. 14:24-7). Mark the
point of the quotation, which is not the deliverance of
Israel, but the glory of God. The Egyptians saw that the
Lord was fighting for Israel, and glorified him (Matt.
5:16), not them! Further, Exodus 14:31 says, 'When
the Israelites saw the great power the Lord displayed
against the Egyptians, the people feared the Lord,
and put their trust in him and in Moses his servant'.
Here are two testimonies to the glory of God: one from
the Egyptians, the other from Israel. All this, then, is
to his glory, and nothing that is ultimately to his glory
comes amiss, however calamitous it may appear to be
at first.

We have referred to Romans 9. Paul there argues that
we must let God be God and not ask impertinent
questions. 'Who are you, O man,to talk back to God? . . .
What if God, choosing to show his wrath and make his
power known, bore with great patience the objects of his
wrath — prepared for destruction? What if he did this to
make the riches of his glory known to the objects of his
mercy, whom he prepared in advance for glory — even us
. . .' (9:20-24) That is the Almighty's business — glory.
Evil only provides the friction to produce it, and when
grace triumphs over every evil thing, what is there to
fear? Nothing, absolutely nothing.

> *Jesus! the Name high over all.*
>   *In hell, or earth, or sky:*
> *Angels and men before it fall.*
> *And devils fear and fly.*

What, then, is the peace of God? A negation? The mere
absence of the undesirable? God forbid! God's peace is a
positive blessing, not a vacuum. But what sort of a
blessing is it? At the very least it consists of

undistraction, which, blessedly, affords complete freedom to enjoy God. We must therefore strive to remain undistracted, not only by evil, but by all that evil would use to distract us. That will include turning aside from some of the highest and best gifts of God. 'The time is short. From now on those who have wives should live as though they had none; those that mourn, as if they did not; those who are happy, as if they were not; those who buy something, as if it were not theirs to keep; those who use the things of the world, as if not engrossed in them. For this world in its present form is passing away ... I am saying this for your own good, not to restrict you, but that you may live in a right way in undivided devotion to the Lord' (1 Cor. 7:29-35).

Spiritual maturity, then, is in sight when we begin to know that freedom from sinful and carnal distraction, high or low, which affords the soul leisure for the enjoyment of God. 'Man's chief end is to glorify God and enjoy him for ever' (*Westminster Shorter Catechism*). Is this in conflict with human duty, or with Christian warfare? Not at all! It is the inspiration of both, and of every good work, and is prior to them all. Without love to Jesus, as the Spirit says to the Ephesians (Rev. 2:1-7), there is nothing. But with it, all things are possible.

Let us end with these words of Jesus, simple and profound: 'I have told you this so that my joy may be in you, and that your joy may be complete', (John 15:11). Note, '*my* joy' becomes '*your* joy'. The promise is nothing less than fulness of joy.

And what is the Psalmist's response to such a sweet challenge? And what is yours, and mine? It ought to be: 'You are my Lord; apart from you I have no good thing ... Lord, you have assigned me my portion and my cup; you have made my lot secure. The boundary lines have fallen for me in pleasant places; surely I have a delightful inheritance ... Therefore my heart is glad and my tongue rejoices; my body also will rest secure ... You have made known to me the path of life; you will fill me with joy in

your presence, with eternal pleasures at your right hand'
(Ps. 16:2,3,5,6,9,11).

This is the voice of spiritual maturity!

APPENDIX 1

See *The Westminster Confession of Faith*, chapter 13, Of Sanctification. See also John Owen, Goold Edition, Vol. III, pp. 386, 388, 465, 488.

APPENDIX 2

See Bunyan's *The Pilgrim's Progress*, Part I, from the place at which Little Faith lies asleep in Dead Man's Lane, to the place where Christian meets with Atheist.

See also in Bunyan's own editions a footnote by Mason where Hope remarks on the cowardice of the three fellows, Faint-heart, Mistrust and Guilt.

See John Owen, Goold Edition. Vol. VI, pp. 190, 191, 193, 194, 203, 204, 212-214.